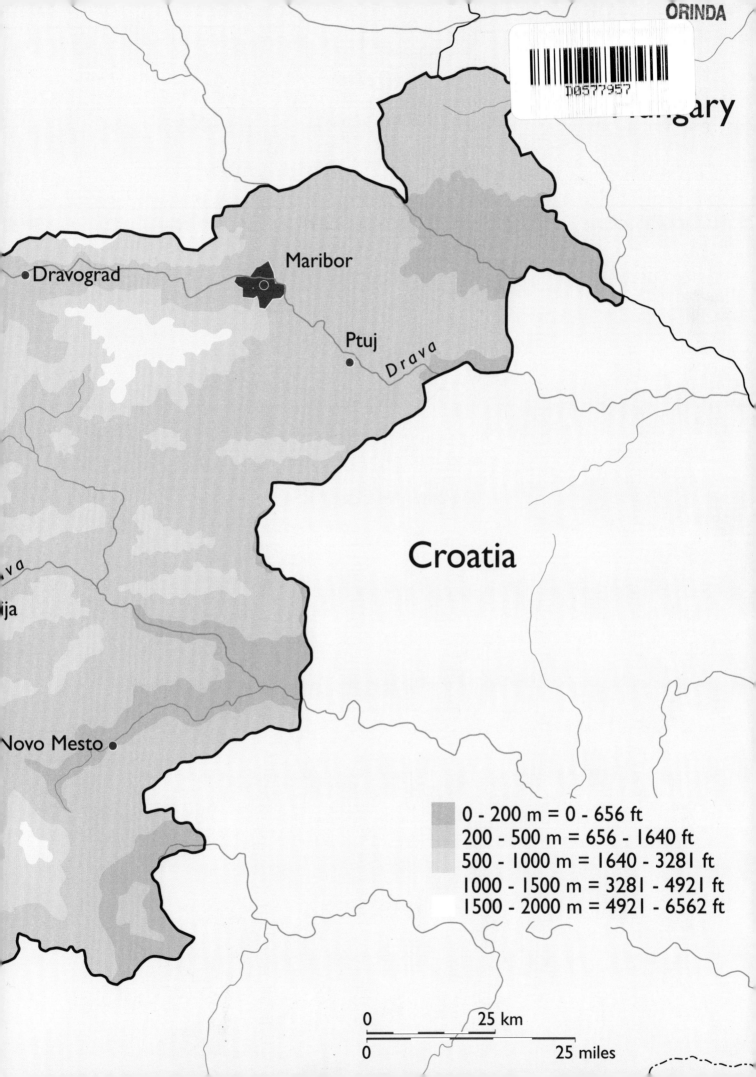

Hungary

Dravograd

Maribor

Ptuj

Drava

Croatia

ava

ija

Novo Mesto

0 - 200 m = 0 - 656 ft
200 - 500 m = 656 - 1640 ft
500 - 1000 m = 1640 - 3281 ft
1000 - 1500 m = 3281 - 4921 ft
1500 - 2000 m = 4921 - 6562 ft

0   25 km

0   25 miles

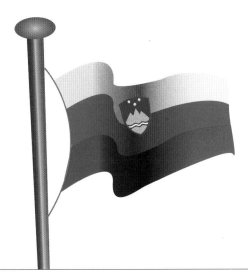

Looking at Europe

Slovenia

Danica Večerić

The Oliver Press, Inc.
Minneapolis

This edition published in 2006 by The Oliver Press, Inc.
Charlotte Square
5707 West 36th Street
Minneapolis, MN 55416-2510

Published by arrangement with KIT Publishers, The Netherlands, and
The Evans Publishing Group, London, UK, 2005

Library of Congress Cataloging-in-Publication Data

Veceric, Danica.
    Slovenia / Danica Veceric.
        p. cm. -- (Looking at Europe)
    Includes index.
    Contents: History -- The country -- Towns and cities -- People and culture -- Education -- Cuisine -- Transportation -- The economy -- Tourism -- Nature -- Slovenia in Europe.
    ISBN 1-881508-74-9
    1. Slovenia--Juvenile literature. I. Title. II. Series.

DR1360.V43 2006
949.73--dc22
                                                                          2006040098

Text: © Danica Veceric 2004
Photographs: Jan Willem Bultje
Translation: Howard Turner
US editing: Holly Day
Design and Layout: Grafisch Ontwerpbureau Agaatsz BNO, Meppel, The Netherlands
Cover: Icon Productions, Minneapolis, USA
Cartography: Armand Haye, Amsterdam, The Netherlands
Production: J & P Far East Productions, Soest, The Netherlands

Picture Credits
Photographs: Slovenian Tourist Board, Ljubljana, Slovenia
p. 5 (b), 13 (b), 15 (t),13 (c), 26, 34, 35, 29, 30 (t), 39 (b):Jan Willem Bultje;
p. 11(t) © Hulton-Deutsch Collection/CORBIS; p. 47(t) © SRDJAN ZIVULOVIC/ Reuters/CORBIS; p. 47(b) © Nikola Solic/Reuters/CORBIS

ISBN 1-881508-74-9
Printed in Singapore
10 09 08 07 06   8 7 6 5 4 3 2 1

Contents

Introduction

Slovenia lies to the south of Central Europe, on the Adriatic coast between Austria, Hungary, Croatia, and Italy. Slovenes sometimes refer to it as the "country on the sunny side of the Alps" because although large parts of it are mountainous, the southwestern coastline enjoys a warm Mediterranean climate.

Although it only became a country in its own right at the end of the twentieth century, Slovene people have lived on this territory continuously since the sixth century. The various political events and territorial aspirations of their stronger neighbors have caused the country's frontiers to change and, as a result, many Slovene communities have been isolated outside its borders in Austria, Italy, and Hungary.

Slovenia lies at the crossroads of four very different European regions, and its landscape and climate vary greatly across the country. It has mountains, lowlands, rolling hills, and beaches. It also has a vast and dramatic limestone landscape, in which the rock has been worn away to result in thousands of landscape features and formations. Among these are underground rivers and lakes, and many caves – some of them hundreds of feet deep.

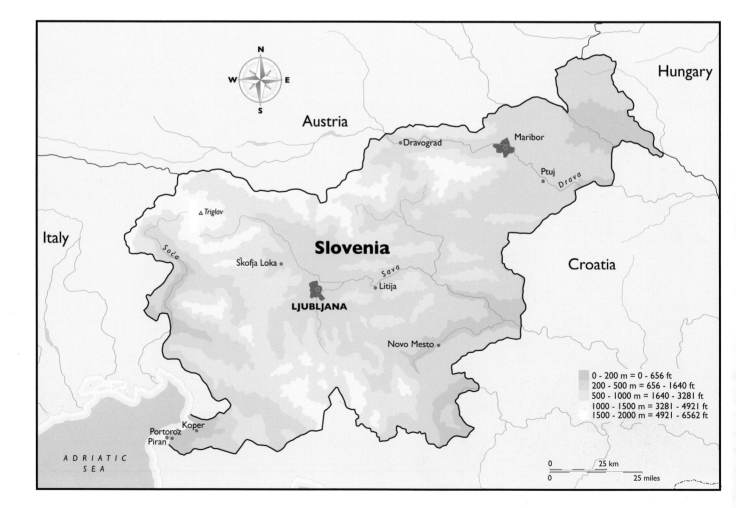

0 - 200 m = 0 - 656 ft
200 - 500 m = 656 - 1640 ft
500 - 1000 m = 1640 - 3281 ft
1000 - 1500 m = 3281 - 4921 ft
1500 - 2000 m = 4921 - 6562 ft

Slovenia is one of the youngest European states. Throughout history, the Slovenian territories have been annexed to other countries. Slovenia was made part of Yugoslavia after the Second World War, and remained so until it was granted independence in 1991.

Slovenia has one of the most stable economies of all the countries that were part of the former Yugoslavia. Others have been affected by war and conflict, but Slovenia has remained peaceful. Since its independence, the country has become a member of several important international organizations, working towards peace, security, economic development, and aid for people in need all over the world. It was accepted as a full member of the United Nations a year after its independence. The country is also a member of NATO, the European Council, and the European Union, which it joined on May 1, 2004.

Tourism has increased since the country gained independence, as more and more people have discovered the mountains, which are ideal for skiing, and the Mediterranean climate on the small strip of coastline on the Adriatic Sea. It may be small, but Slovenia is one of the most varied and interesting countries in Europe.

▲ The Opera House in Slovenia's capital, Ljubljana

▼ Many villages in Slovenia are built on hilltops. This is the village of Štanjel.

History

The Slovenes are descendants of the Slavic tribes that migrated to the eastern Alps in the second half of the sixth century AD. By the end of the seventh century AD, they occupied the area that is now Slovenia as well as territories throughout the Alps, all the way to the River Danube in what is now Vienna.

▼ *Predjama Castle is built into the rock. The present building dates from the sixteenth century, but there has been a fortress here since 1201.*

The Slovenes banished most of the existing settlers, including the Celts, and became neighbors to the Bavarians, Longobards, Avars, and Byzantines, with whom they often fought. The "state" that the Slovenes established on this territory was called Karantania. The center of Karantania was located at Karnburg, close to what is now Klagenfurt in southern Austria. The state was governed by a duke, who was installed following a special ceremony, at which he had to swear to be a fair and judicious ruler, and to ensure the well-being of his people and lands.

Martin Krpan

Martin Krpan is a Slovenian folk hero. He made his living by smuggling salt – a very costly item – from the coast of what is now Austria to his village in Slovenia. He had a reputation for great strength and, although his smuggling activities were illegal, the Austrian emperor called upon Martin to help defeat the Turkish giant Brdavs, who had killed many men, including the emperor's son. Martin succeeded in killing this man, whom so many feared. The emperor was grateful and offered Martin great riches and even his daughter's hand in marriage, but the empress would not agree to this. Martin was angry at her ingratitude, and said he would never come to Vienna's aid again. Instead, he was granted a license to legally transport salt to Slovenia.

▲ *Martin Krpan fighting Brdavs*

In the eighth century, Christianity began to spread across the region. The Karantanians learned about it from their neighbors and eventually adopted the religion themselves. The spread of Christianity helped in the development of the written word, and this led to the creation of the Freising manuscripts in the tenth century. These are the oldest-known written records in the Slovenian language.

Germanic rule

In AD 748, the Karantanians lost their independence to their stronger Germanic neighbors, who became their overlords. During the time of Germanic rule, the German language was widely used, and the Slovenian language was only preserved among the peasant population.

▲ *Otočec Castle stands on an islet in the Krka River, in southern Slovenia. It dates from the thirteenth century.*

In the ninth century, new enemies appeared on the borders of Karantania – the Hungarians. To make it easier to defend the territory, Karantania was divided into several smaller regions. Five main territories emerged, and remained as separate regions until 1918: Styria, Carinthia, Carniola, Gorivka, and Primorska. These regions were occupied by Slovenes and Germanic peoples.

By the Middle Ages, Slovenian territories were ruled by important feudal families such as the Spanheims, Babensburgs and, in the fourteenth century, the powerful Habsburg family. For a few decades, the Celje dukes took over the territories, but when the last Duke of Celje, Ulrik II, died in 1456, most of the Slovenian lands fell completely under Habsburg rule.

Turkish attacks

In the second half of the fifteenth century, Turks began raiding Slovenia. They pillaged and plundered, and many of the inhabitants were either killed or taken into slavery. Small boys were carried off to Turkey to be raised as janissaries – the toughest of Turkish soldiers.

At first, the Turks only plundered Slovenia, but by the middle of the fifteenth century, the raids had turned into an attempted invasion. They were stopped by the Hungarian king, Matija Korvin. The Slovene people remember him in folksongs and legends as King Matjaž.

▲ *A likeness of Primož Trubar, who helped spread the Slovenian language through his books*

Protestantism

In the sixteenth century, a new religious movement spread from the surrounding countries. Protestantism – literally a movement that "protested" against the corruption of the Catholic Church – was sweeping through Europe.

In Slovenia, the leader of the Protestant movement was Primož Trubar, who wrote the first true Slovenian books – a catechism (a book about the principles of Christianity) and a dictionary. Trubar also encouraged other writers, and this resulted in more books in the Slovenian language. Jurij Dalmatin translated the Bible into Slovenian, and Hieronim Megiser compiled the first multi-language dictionary, bringing the Slovenian language to the attention of other European nations. During this period, the first printing business was established in the capital, Ljubljana.

▼ *The old town center of Piran, with a statue of the composer Giuseppe Tartini, who was born here in 1692*

The golden age

From the sixteenth century onward, Slovenia began to develop economically. Factories were built, the rivers were busy with traffic, and a transportation system was established. During the eighteenth century, many reforms were introduced by Empress Maria Theresa, wife of the Holy Roman Emperor, and life in the region began to improve for the peasant population. In particular, the empress insisted that all children should go to school. This was a golden period for Slovenia. Poets and authors started writing in the Slovenian language, and the people began to be more aware of their history and culture.

The French emperor Napoleon wanted to reduce the power of the Habsburgs, and in 1809 he seized what he called the Illyrian Provinces, which included present-day Slovenia. Napoleon allowed the Slovenes to use their own language in schools and workplaces. Even after the French gave up control of the lands, many of the reforms they had put in place in education, law, and, administration, were maintained.

▲ *Empress Maria Theresa*

The Illyrian Provinces were returned to the Habsburgs in 1814 and remained under their rule for the next century.

Until 1848, the Slovenes did not use the name Slovenia for their country. Instead, they called themselves Carniolans, Styrians, or Carinthians, according to the area from which they came. The rulers of the Slovenian territories were Germans, Hungarians, and Italians. The official language was German, and Slovenian was only spoken in the countryside.

In 1848, revolution swept across Europe, including Slovenia. There was demand for social and political reform. In Vienna, Slovene intellectuals wrote the first political program, entitled *Unified Slovenia*. In this program they demanded that the Slovenian language receive equal status to German, and that Carniola, Carinthia, Styria, and a fourth region, called Primorska, should unify under the name Slovenia.

▶ *The former monastery of Kostanjevica, founded in the seventeenth century*

▲ *Mementoes of the First World War can be found in the museum at Kobarid in western Slovenia.*

The First World War

At the beginning of the First World War (1914–18), Slovenia was still part of the Austro-Hungarian Empire. Young Slovenian men were drafted into the Austrian army. One of the European front lines during the war was the Soča front, alongside the River Soča in the Alps. Here, fighting took place between the Austrians and the Italians. A great number of young Slovenian soldiers lost their lives in this campaign. The civilian inhabitants of the region suffered starvation and many died from disease. Thousands more were forced to flee as the battles raged.

During the war, some political parties called for the southern Slav nations to join together under one flag. In 1918, following the disintegration of the Austro-Hungarian Empire, the Slovenes, Croats, and Serbs declared themselves an independent country on December 1, 1918. They called this the Kingdom of Serbs, Croats, and Slovenes. In 1929, this country was renamed the Kingdom of Yugoslavia.

◄ *The Soča River in the Alps, on the border between Slovenia and Italy, was the front line in this region during the First World War.*

The Second World War

In the first months of the Second World War (1939–45), the Kingdom of Yugoslavia remained relatively unaffected by the fighting going on elsewhere in Europe. However, on April 6, 1941, the area was attacked by armies of Germans, Italians, and Hungarians. They wreaked havoc, burning down villages and sending inhabitants to concentration camps. By the time the war ended, much of the country's infrastructure had been destroyed and its population displaced. The Slovenes, Croats, Serbs, Montenegrins, and Macedonians created a new country called the Federal Republic of Yugoslavia. Joseph Tito, a military leader who had been wounded in fighting against the Germans, became the country's prime minister (and later president). At first, Tito's policies were very much in line with those of the communist Soviet Union. Soon, however, he began to move away from this, and Yugoslavia split with the Soviet Union in 1948. Tito strongly disapproved of the Russian invasions of Hungary in 1956 and Czechoslovakia in 1968.

After Tito's death in 1980, no one could decide how to run a country that was inhabited by so many different nations. The republic continued for another 10 years, but several of the regions wanted to become independent states. Slovenia declared independence on June 25, 1991. In response, Yugoslavia mobilized its army, but pressure from the European Union ensured that the battle lasted only 10 days. Slovenia had won its independence. In May of 1992, the country was admitted to the United Nations, and this has been followed by membership in several other international organizations.

▲ German soldiers in a Slovenian village on the Drava River, in 1941

Joseph Tito

Tito was born Joseph Broz on May 25, 1892, to a Croat father and Slovene mother in the village of Kumrovec, in present-day Croatia. During the First World War, he fought in the Austrian (Habsburg) army, and was taken prisoner and sent to Russia. There he witnessed the overthrow of the Russian tsar and the introduction of the communist government. In 1920, Tito returned to Zagreb – now in the new Kingdom of Serbs, Croats, and Slovenes – and in 1928 he became secretary of the Communist Party, which was forbidden at that time. He was arrested and imprisoned many times. He was not put off, however, and in 1937 he began to reorganize the country's Communist Party. Throughout the Second World War, Tito led the resistance against the German and Italian occupiers. During this period, the Communist Party became the most powerful political group in the region, and at the end of the war Tito became the leader of the Federal Republic of Yugoslavia.

▼ Joseph Tito, the first president of the Federal Republic of Yugoslavia

The country

Slovenia is one of the smaller countries in Europe, both in terms of size and population. It covers an area of about 7,800 square miles and it has a population of just over two million. It has dramatic mountains and fertile lowlands, tranquil lakes and bustling cities, inland rivers and sunny beaches.

The countryside in Slovenia is diverse. Four European landscapes meet in this region – the Alps, the Pannonian Lowlands, the Dinar mountain range, and the Mediterranean.

Three Alpine ranges occupy the northwestern part of Slovenia – the Julian Alps, the Kamniško-Savinjske Alps and the Karavanken Mountains. The highest peak is Triglav (9,396 feet). There are also several lakes in this region, including Lake Bled, Lake Bohinj, and the seven Triglav lakes. Numerous rivers flow down from the Alps, forming rapids, waterfalls, and narrow gorges.

▼ *Lake Bled, in Slovenia's Alpine region,*
is renowned for its beauty.

The Pannonian Lowlands continue from Slovenia into Hungary and Croatia. Here, numerous hills are mixed with valleys and plains. The hills are covered with forests and are ideal for the cultivation of vines and fruit trees. Wheat, corn, sugar beets, and potatoes are grown in the fertile fields.

The Dinar mountain range starts in the southern part of Slovenia and continues along the Adriatic coast. The landscape features limestone, which may be found both on the surface and below the ground, as well as in underground caves and lakes. The limestone plateaus are covered with woods, many of which are beautifully preserved, particularly those in Kočevski Rog.

Slovenia is a coastal country. It lies on the Adriatic coast, which is a part of the larger Mediterranean Sea. The coast offers the people of Slovenia a "window on the world," because ships from many other countries can reach the port of Koper here. The warmth of the Adriatic coast makes it popular with tourists during the summer months, when the sea temperature can reach a pleasant 80°F. In the winter, it cools to 55°F. The sea is also an important source of salt, which is harvested via salt-pans. In the Bay of Trieste, the Adriatic Sea reaches its northernmost point. The coastal territories have a warm climate and evergreen vegetation.

▲ *The Triglav lakes lie in the national park of the same name. Each of the seven lakes has a different mineral composition and, therefore, a different color.*

▲ *The most famous salt-pans are the ones at Secovlje.*

◀ *The Pannonian Lowlands consist of flat plains, valleys, and tree-covered hills.*

Rivers

Slovenia is a land of water. The best-known rivers are the Sava, Drava, and Soča. The poet Simon Gregorčič wrote about the Soča: "You are beautiful, the clear daughter of the mountains, graceful in your natural beauty...."

The river Drava rises in neighboring Austria. Because the water in the river is plentiful throughout the year, it is used by hydroelectric power stations.

The Sava is the longest river in Slovenia. It continues its course into Croatia and then flows into the River Danube.

In the past, all three of these rivers were used for transporting goods, including timber, coal, and wheat, to various cities within Slovenia.

▼ *The Drava River near Ptuj, in the northeast of the country*

▲ *The Soča River is regarded as the most beautiful river in Slovenia because of its clear blue-green water.*

There are several other rivers in Slovenia that are just as important. The Ljubljanica River runs through the capital, Ljubljana. It is also known as "the river of seven names," because it is known by different names at certain points along its course, including where it runs underground.

Most rivers that alternate between running above the surface and then disappearing underground are found in limestone landscapes. In such areas the intermittent rivers have dissolved the limestone under the ground and have created impressive underground caves. There are many landscape features like this in Slovenia.

Numerous rivers and streams have formed narrow valleys, gorges, and river beds, which can reach 230 feet in depth. The most dramatic gorges can be found on the rivers Radovna, Koritnica, Tolminka, and Soča. Waterfalls are also important tourist spots. The most picturesque waterfalls are Savica at Bohinj Lake, Peričnik in the Vrata Valley, Boka on the Soča River, and Rinka in the Savinjske Alps.

▲ *The Ljubljanica as it runs through the capital city, Ljubljana*

▶ *These caves near Škocjan have been formed by the river water wearing away the surrounding limestone.*

◄ *A mountain-pass in the Julian Alps connects the towns of Rateč and Podkoren.*

Lakes

Slovenia has numerous lakes of different origins. In the Alps, there are glacial lakes, which are the remains of great glaciers that covered the mountain region during the Ice Age. Lakes Bhinj and Bled have glacial origins, and both usually freeze during the winter. In the summer, however, they are warm enough to swim in.

The Cerknica Lake is a fascinating place to visit. From the autumn to spring it holds water, but in the summer, when there is not enough rainfall to maintain the water levels, the lake empties. The water runs through large sinkholes in the limestone and leaves the bottom of the lake covered with grass.

The water in the Wild Lake near Idrija comes from a spring, which flows on into deep caves. There are also several ox-bow lakes, which emerge on river bends. The most famous ones can be found on the River Mura, and many birds make their homes here.

▼ *Lake Bohinj*

▲ *The massive caves at Postojna*

Caves

Slovenia has a wonderful series of caves with magnificent limestone features. Approximately 7,500 caves have been discovered in Slovenia, but for safety reasons only a few of them are open to the general public. The Postojna caves are famous worldwide and feature numerous galleries and chambers with huge stalactites. The Škocjan caves, which have underground canyons up to 295 feet high, are now protected by the organization UNESCO. The Križna cave is renowned for its underground lakes. Numerous animal species have made their home in the caves, ranging from bats and crabs, to spiders and the cave salamander (*Proteus anguinus*), a species of amphibian.

◀ *Stalactites grow very slowly — on average, less than an inch every century.*

Climate

Like the landscape, Slovenia's climate is diverse. In the mountainous regions, the climate is cold and is often referred to as an "Alpine climate." The winters are long, cold, and snowy. However, this part of the country is ideal for skiing, and there are wonderful slopes on Pohorje, in the vicinity of Kranjska Gora, on Kanin and Krvavec. Summers in the mountains can be pleasantly warm – ideal for hikers who want to explore the mountain peaks. In the summer, the water in the lakes also gets agreeably warm, and visitors can swim here in the natural environment.

Along the Adriatic coast, the climate in the summer is hot, and there is not much rainfall. Winters are short and fairly mild. The temperature rarely reaches freezing. Because the Adriatic Sea – which is a part of the Mediterranean Sea – has a great influence upon the climate, this climate is known as "Mediterranean." From the limestone plateaus, strong winds blow towards the sea, and have been known to reach speeds of up to 125 mph.

▲ *Summertime on the Adriatic coast is hot and sunny.*

The rest of Slovenia has a continental climate. Here, the summers are long and hot, and the winters long and cold. Sometimes, the hot summer months produce less than an ideal amount of rainfall, leaving Slovenia affected by drought.

▶ *Lake Bled in the winter*

Towns and cities

In comparison to other European towns and cities, those in Slovenia are quite small. Only 15 of them have more than 10,000 inhabitants. However, the towns are not full of high-rise blocks, and they have plenty of parks and gardens. Generally, Slovenian towns are pleasant places to live or visit.

▲ *An aerial view of the Slovenian capital, Ljubljana*

The reason that Slovenian towns are so small is that many people still prefer to live in the countryside. Here, they can have their own houses rather than flats or apartments, and they can own more land. Farming villages are still common in certain areas of Slovenia. There are even a few farms located high up in the Alps. There are very few traditional farmhouses left nowadays – most of them have been replaced by modern houses, which offer greater comfort. Some old houses have been turned into museums, which show how people lived in the past. Among the particular architectural curiosities in the country are the Slovenian haysheds, where people would store hay once it had been harvested. Painted beehives are also an interesting feature of the countryside.

Industry and other activities are concentrated in the towns, and workers usually commute daily to the towns from the smaller settlements that have been established in the surrounding areas.

◀ *A traditional hayshed in the Slovenian countryside*

Ljubljana

Ljubljana is the capital of Slovenia and is its cultural, political, and economic center. This is where the president, the parliament, the constitutional and supreme courts, and most embassies are located. In addition to its primary and secondary schools, Ljubljana has a university. The UNESCO International Center for Chemical Studies is also based in Ljubljana. The center of cultural activities can be found in the complex of halls and exhibition pavilions in Cankarjev Dom. Theaters, opera, orchestral halls, and museums, as well as the national and university libraries, are all located in the center of the city.

A great many tourists visit Ljubljana because of its cultural and historic places of interest, for sport, and trade fairs.

▼ *Many brightly colored houses face the River Ljublijanica in the capital.*

▶ *The dragon is the symbol of Ljubljana. The inhabitants of the city are nicknamed "zmajceki," which means "little dragons."*

Koper

Koper is a coastal town located on the
Gulf of Trieste. It is Slovenia's major fishing
port and is also a center for salt mining.
The town spent more than 500 years under
the rule of the Venetians, and when the
Republic of Venice was dissolved, ownership
of the town passed to Austria and then
Italy, before becoming part of Yugoslavia
and subsequently Slovenia.

Ptuj

Ptuj, in northeastern Slovenia, is the oldest town in the country. It dates back to Roman times, although
much of the present look and feel of the town dates from the Middle Ages, when it experienced a rise
in wealth and prosperity. There are plenty of museums and galleries in Ptuj, as well as the fascinating
archeological remains from ancient times. Roman remains can also be found in Ljubljana, Celje, and
Ajdovščina.

Škofja Loka

One of the best-preserved medieval towns in Slovenia is Škofja Loka, which was founded by the
bishops of Freiburg in AD 973. In the fourteenth century, a town wall was built, with five entrance
gates, each one guarded by a watchtower. Much of the wall remains today. The town also has a castle
and several old churches.

Maribor

Maribor is another town with a long history – people were living here on the banks of the Drava River
as early as the twelfth century. Although it is now an important industrial center, with a number of
factories, there are several historical buildings still standing, including a twelfth-century Gothic cathedral
and a fifteenth-century castle.

MESTNA OBČINA
MARIBOR
Dobrodošli Welcome

▶ The city of Maribor on the Drava River

People and culture

In Slovenia, just over two million people live in an area of about 7,800 square miles. The population density is lower than in most European countries and there are, on average, 256 people per square mile.

The population density is influenced by Slovenia's diverse landscape and climate. The number of inhabitants also depends on industrial growth. After the Second World War, large numbers of people moved to the towns and cities from the villages. Population density is also influenced by natural population growth, which has declined in the last few decades because the economic and social climate has been difficult.

Throughout its history, Slovenia has experienced several periods when large numbers of people moved away from the region. The largest migrations were caused by difficult economic conditions. Major migrations took place at the end of the nineteenth century and the beginning of the twentieth century, with Slovenes mainly migrating to the USA and Australia. After the Second World War, a large number of people left to seek temporary work in the more economically developed countries of Germany, Switzerland, Belgium, and France. However, many workers from regions such as Serbia, Bosnia Herzegovina, and Croatia moved to Slovenia.

Ethnic minorities

Around 88 percent of the population are Slovene. The rest are minorities. The two main minority groups in Slovenia are Italians, who live in the Koper area, and Hungarians, who live in the Prekmurje region. Minorities have the same rights as Slovenes, and can freely use their own national symbols and establish schools and other organizations in order to preserve their ethnic identity.

Minorities are are also free to develop their own economic, cultural, and scientific research activities. Muslims, Serbs, Albanians, Macedonians, Croats, and Montenegrins from what was once Yugoslavia have moved into larger industrial cities in Slovenia. There are also a number of Roma, or Gypsies, in the country. They largely live in the Prekmurje region, the Dolenjska region, and in Bela Krajina.

◀ Locals and tourists wander through the town square in Maribor.

Language

The official language is Slovenian, a south-Slavic language related to Serbian and Croatian. It is written in the Latin alphabet, but uses many diacritic marks (accents). Hungarian, German, and Italian are the tongues spoken by minority groups. These languages are given equal importance with Slovenian.

Religion

The most widespread religion in Slovenia is Roman Catholicism (around 58 percent of the population), followed by Orthodox Christianity and Islam (each around 2.4 percent). Protestant faiths and other religions are also practiced. Slovenia's constitution grants everyone the right to follow their religion of choice. Most of the churches in Slovenia are Roman Catholic, but areas with other religious groups have their own buildings for worship.

Some Slovene words

Good morning	*Dobro jutro*
Please	*Prosim*
Thank you	*Hvala*
Yes	*Da*
No	*Ne*
Good evening	*Dober večer*
Goodbye	*Na svidenje*

1	*ena*
2	*dva*
3	*tri*
4	*štiri*
5	*pet*
6	*šest*
7	*sedem*
8	*osem*
9	*devet*
10	*deset*

State symbols

The main state symbols in Slovenia are the flag, the coat of arms, the national anthem, and the country's currency. The Slovenian flag consists of three equal horizontal bands of white, blue, and red. The Slovenian seal, a shield with the image of Triglav, Slovenia's highest peak, in white against a blue background is at the center. Beneath it are two wavy blue lines depicting seas and rivers, and above it are three six-pointed stars arranged in an inverted triangle. This symbol is taken from the coat of arms of the Counts of Celje used in the fourteenth and early fifteenth centuries. The seal is located in the upper hoist, or mast side, of the flag, centered in the white and blue bands.

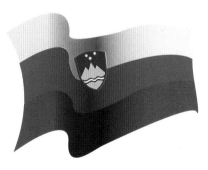

▲ *Slovenia's national flag*

◄ *The church of St. Francis in Ljubljana*

▶ *A fragment of the poem* Zdravljica *by France Prešeren, in the poet's own hand. In the nineteenth century, the poem was removed from a volume of Prešeren's poems by the state censor.*

France Prešeren's poem *Zdravljica* was adopted as Slovenia's national anthem in in 1990. It speaks of democracy and the people's desire for peace:

> *God's blessing on all nations,*
> *Who long and work for that bright day,*
> *When o'er earth's habitations*
> *No war, no strife shall hold its sway;*
> *Who long to see*
> *That all men free*
> *No more shall foes, but neighbors be.*

The currency in Slovenia is the tolar (SIT). There are around 200 tolars in one U.S. dollar. There are 100 stotins to a tolar.

▲ *Although the official currency is still the Slovenian tolar, the country plans to adopt the euro in 2007.*

France Prešeren

France Prešeren (1800–49) is one of the greatest poets in the history of Slovenia. He was a follower of the Romantic Movement, a period in which emotions found their way into many artistic forms. Prešeren did not have far to look for inspiration. His unhappy private life was a rich source, as he was an alcoholic and forever in love with unattainable women. He died young and penniless from excessive drinking. There are two important recurring themes in Prešeren's work: his desire that his country should be free, and his great, unrequited passion for Julija Primic, the daughter of a rich merchant from Ljubljana, who thought Prešeren too lowly for his daughter. His desire for his country's freedom is the subject of his famous poem, *Zdravljica* ("The Toast"), which Prešeren wrote in 1844. The poem is an impassioned plea for an independent Slovenia, inspired by the ideals of the French Revolution – freedom, equality, and brother-hood. In his poem, Prešeren tried to stress the importance of peaceful relations between the various nations and the right all peoples have to freedom. For Slovenes, France Prešeren is a national hero – the national Day of Culture is held on the anniversary of his death (February 8), and the most prestigious Slovenian Arts Prize is named after him.

Health

Slovenes are health conscious and enjoy many sports – tennis, swimming, cycling, and skiing. Alternative therapies and yoga are also popular.

Despite this, Slovenes suffer from the same illnesses and diseases as people in the rest of Europe. Cancer remains the most common disease, and there have been a number of cases of HIV and AIDS in the country, although a preventative program has been set up to restrict its spread. Hospitals can be found in every large city, and the capital, Ljubljana, has several clinics. Health centers take care of the everyday illnesses.

▲ This health spa has medicinal springs, which are thought to have therapeutic properties.

▼ A television program being recorded

Media

Slovenia has a national television station (TV Slovenia), two commercial television stations, and 12 smaller local television stations. International television programs can be viewed via satellite stations, and a wide selection of satellite and cable channels are available. The country also receives programs from all over the world.

In addition, Slovenia has a large number of radio stations. Almost every town has its own local station. Apart from news and entertainment, radio and television offer educational services.

▶ *The market in Ljubljana. Many people buy their fresh fruit, vegetables, cheese, and other foods from outdoor markets.*

▼ *There are large department stores in the big towns.*

Shopping

Most towns in Slovenia have large shopping centers, with shops similar to other towns and cities in Europe. These shops offer food and products from all over the world. Just about every town has a market where people purchase fruit and vegetables, and other fresh produce.

Fast-food restaurants are very popular with young people, and most towns have them. There are also many Chinese restaurants, and several others offering cuisine from countries all over the world, such as France, Spain, and Mexico.

◀ *A group of singers and dancers from Bela Krajina*

Entertainment

Young people generally prefer to spend their free time in pubs and clubs. A great number of them attend dance schools, where they learn how to dance Latin American dances, hip-hop, and other modern dance styles. Many people visit movie theaters to see international films, which quickly find their way to Slovenia. On the weekends, various activities are held in the large shopping centers. Many like to visit the theater, opera, and concerts to see and hear local and international singers. On major public holidays, numerous parties are organized in towns and villages, which present opportunities for people to dance, have fun, and socialize.

▼ *Skiing is a national pastime in Slovenia. Locals and tourists alike enjoy the fine snow on the Alpine slopes.*

◄ National holidays are causes of colorful celebration in Slovenia. People join their neighbors in the streets, and often fairs and other events are held.

Festivals

There are a number of festivals and public holidays in Slovenia. There is the Celebration of the Uprising in April, when people remember the day that the country rose against German occupation during the Second World War. Slovenes also celebrate their own independence in December.

Government

Slovenia declared its independence on June 25, 1991. On December 23 the same year, the Assembly of the Republic of Slovenia adopted the Constitution of the Republic of Slovenia, which outlined the basis for a new democratic state. All legislation in Slovenia must be in legal agreement with the principles and articles of the constitution. The constitution emphasizes the country's belief in universal respect for human rights and basic freedoms for all people.

The government is made up of three major components: the legislature, the executive, and the judiciary. The legislature is represented by a parliament with 90 members, which agrees on new legislation, and the national council, which offers advice to the parliament.

▲ A brass band marches through the streets on a public holiday.

The executive is represented by the government and the president. The government is responsible for making sure that legislation is enforced. This means that the government takes care of education, health care, the police force, the armed forces, social security, and many other aspects of everyday life in Slovenia. The president is helped in his duties by his ministers. Judges elect their own leaders.

The president represents the Republic of Slovenia at home and abroad as the head of state and calls elections, presents state awards and also acts as supreme commander of the armed forces. The president is elected directly by the people.

In Slovenia, there is also an ombudsman (an office that helps people with complaints) for human rights, which protects the citizens of the Republic of Slovenia in their relations with the state authorities and public officials. The ombudsman is elected by parliament after a recommendation made by the president.

▶ The House of Parliament in Ljubljana

Education

Education is compulsory for all children between the ages of six and 15 in Slovenia. Almost all the schools are state-run, and there are only a few private institutions. Schools are funded by the government.

Elementary school lasts for nine years – the duration of compulsory education in Slovenia. Although the education itself is free, parents have to buy textbooks and other learning materials.

There must be at least 28 pupils in each class of elementary school, so less-populated areas of the country often have classes made up of pupils of different ages. In the first four years, classes are taught by one teacher, but after this, different teachers offer lessons in different subjects.

▲ *A school in Ravne na Kasoškem*

▼ *A sign warns that a school is up ahead and drivers should slow down.*

These boys are walking to school in the rain. They go to elementary school, which lasts nine years. The education system in Slovenia has proved successful. A number of schools have attained the status of a "healthy school." This means that they have been recognized for making a special effort to create a caring learning environment. In particular, they provide their pupils with healthy meals and teach them to respect the natural environment.

Higher education

At the end of elementary school, pupils take exams and receive a diploma if they pass all their subjects. This diploma allows them to go on to further education in the form of secondary schools, either general or vocational. The marks pupils get in their exams are important, particularly those in math, Slovenian, and a foreign language. At secondary schools, children can enroll on either three- or four-year courses in continued general education, or in specific subjects that will train them for a profession.

There are more exams at the end of secondary school, after which students can go on to the university as undergraduates and later as postgraduates if they want to. There are two universities in Slovenia: Ljubljana University (the largest) and the University of Technology in Maribor.

Slovenia has an efficient education system: there are enough schools to accommodate all children, and the facilities are good. Nearly 80 percent of the adult population has a secondary-school diploma, and around 10 percent has a university degree. Education is equally available to both sexes.

▶ Students at the University of Technology in Maribor at work on a project.

Cuisine

Slovenian cuisine is as diverse as the country's landscape, and each region has several traditional dishes. Slovenian food is typically very simple but tasty. Most recipes have their origins in rural cooking.

The Slovenes eat a lot of sauerkraut (pickled cabbage) and black pudding. Black pudding is a sausage made of pork and pig's blood, sometimes filled with rice.

Other traditional dishes include boiled buckwheat mash, Idrija *žlikrofi* – potato balls made with herbs and spices, and wrapped in a thin dough. Bread is much loved by the Slovenes and is served at almost every meal. The best bread is baked in a open-fire oven, and is often made of corn, buckwheat, or wheat flour. Nearly every region of Slovenia has its own speciality bread.

Meat

Pork is the most widely eaten meat in Slovenia. Sausages and ham are particular favorites, and there are several regional meat soups. Along the Adriatic coast, legs of pork dried in the open air are a speciality.

◄ *Pork meats, such as ham and sausages, are eaten all over the country.*

Fish

Fish dishes are popular in Slovenia, particularly along the coast. Shellfish and bluefish, which are caught in the Adriatic Sea, are specialities of the region along the coast. Freshwater fish are also abundant in the rivers and lakes in Slovenia, and restaurants throughout the country offer a range of delicious fish dishes on their menus.

Slow food

A recent fashion in food in Slovenia is called "slow food." A typical meal can take place at a restaurant or at home among friends and family. There can be as many as nine courses at a "slow-food" meal, and these are usually traditional dishes. Everyone takes their time over the meal, and often enjoys a different type of wine with each course.

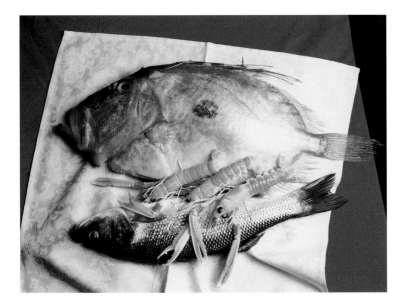

▲ *Many kinds of fish can be found in the country. Some are cooked to traditional Slovenian recipes, while others are influenced by the cuisine of Slovenia's neighboring countries.*

Drink

There are vineyards all across Slovenia, and the tradition of wine-making dates back to Roman times. Because of the country's varied climates – from the Alps to the Mediterranean – many different wines are produced, some of which are gaining a good reputation elsewhere in the world.

▶ *A wine-cellar with large wooden barrels, in which the wine is fermented*

▼ *Thanks to the mild climate, many kinds of fruit are grown.*

▶ *Potica is a favorite sweet dish in Slovenia.*

Dessert

At large celebrations, desserts are prepared. The most popular are various types of pastries, such as potica. Potica is an old Slovenian dish first mentioned in print in 1689. Potica, a hearty treat, is baked in round earthenware pots and can be filled with nuts, poppy seeds, cottage cheese, bacon bits, dried fruit, or tarragon.

The oldest of all desserts are the Slovenian honey pastries, which are baked and sold as bread in the shape of hearts. At large-scale celebrations, these honey hearts are exchanged by lovers.

Recipe for potica

Ingredients for the dough
2 pounds white flour, 2 tablespoons yeast, 4 egg yolks, 1 ¼ cup warm milk, ½ cup butter or margarine, 1 teaspoon of salt, 2 teaspoons of sugar

Ingredients for the filling
1 ½ pounds ground nuts, 7 ounces honey, ¼ cup sugar, ¾ cup milk, 1 egg, a dash of cinnamon

Mix the yeast with a teaspoon of sugar and two tablespoons of flour. Add the salt and ¼ cup of milk to the mixture and then leave it in a warm place to rise. Sift the rest of the flour and butter or margarine into a mixing bowl. Make a hole in the center and add the beaten egg yolks, the rest of the warm milk, and the risen yeast that you mixed earlier. Beat the dough until bubbles appear and it starts to come away from the edge of the bowl easily. Knead it for five minutes, cover it with a clean cloth, and leave it in a warm place to rise.

In the meantime, make the filling. The ground nuts should be scalded with hot milk and the honey should be heated so that it is runny, then added to the nuts. Next, add a bit of cinnamon. Into the slightly cooled filling, add two eggs. Roll the dough out to form a layer, about a quarter-inch thick, and cover it evenly with the filling. Roll it tightly and place it on a greased baking pan and let it rise again. Before putting it in the oven, coat it lightly with beaten eggs and then bake it for 60 minutes at 325°F. Cool the baked roll in the mold for at least 15 minutes, take it out, sprinkle it with sugar, and cover it with a napkin to cool completely.

Transportation

Due to its geographical position in Europe, Slovenia is criss-crossed by many important transportation routes, linking several European countries to the Near East. Even in pre-Roman times, numerous nations crossed this territory and mingled and traded with each other.

Slovenia could be considered the place where Eastern and Western Europe meet. Almost everyone traveling from Austria to Croatia or from Italy to Hungary by road passes through the Slovenian capital, Ljubljana.

Road and railway transportation is increasing across Slovenian territory. This has resulted because of the economic growth of the Eastern European countries that trade with the West across Slovenia. Many highways are currently under construction to provide a faster and more efficient road-transportation system.

◀ *Postojna Railway Station*

Railways

Slovenia has 750 miles of railway tracks, and all the larger Slovenian cities have railway connections. The first railway was built in 1857 and ran from Vienna, through Ljubljana, to Trieste. Many of the railways are quite old, but the rail system is efficient, and trains are one of the most convenient ways of traveling around Slovenia.

Public transport

All the larger cities are connected by bus and rail routes. However, people still prefer to use private cars because this is often the fastest and most comfortable way of traveling around the country. This has resulted in traffic problems around the larger cities and towns, especially those that don't have many parking lots.

Pollution is also increasing because of emissions from automobile exhaust. To solve this problem, steps are being taken to modernize city and suburban public-transportation systems.

▼ *The main international airport at Brnik*

Aviation

Brnik Airport is the main international airport in Slovenia. A smaller airport for tourists is located in Portoroz. The national air carrier is Adria Airways, whose routes mainly connect with European cities. Sport aviation in the form of gliding is a popular activity in Slovenia.

Shipping

The largest industrial port is located in Koper. Here, ships dock from all over the world. Cargo is unloaded and transferred to trucks and trains. The port of Koper is also used by Austria, Hungary, the Czech Republic, and Slovakia, as they are all landlocked countries without ports of their own.

◀ *The port of Koper*

▼ *In tourist resorts on the coast, there are marinas where it is possible to dock sailing or motor boats. This is the marina in Portoro.*

The economy

Throughout the last century, Slovenia's economic system has been through many changes. Although industry is the most important element of the economy, the country now has good trade relations with many European countries.

Slovenia trades mostly with other countries in the European Union, especially Germany, Italy, Austria, and France. However, economic relations with other countries are also improving. In particular, there is greater co-operation with some of the countries that were part of the former Yugoslavia, former republics of the Soviet Union, and the United States of America.

A growing number of countries are showing an interest in the Slovenian economy. The highest level of investment has come from Austria, France, Germany, and Italy.

▲ *A wine-grower pruning his vines*

▼ *Cultivating vines and making wine is an important part of the Slovenian economy.*

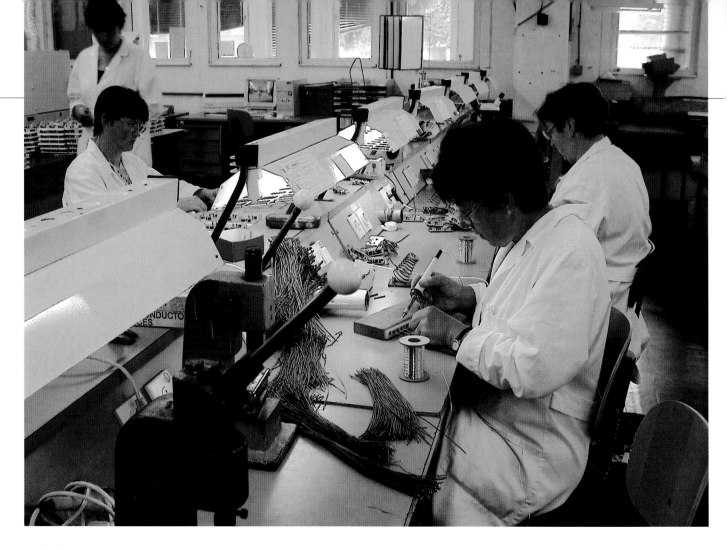

▲ *The production of semiconductors in the Tovarna plant*

The largest Slovene exporters

Revoz – production and marketing of cars
Gorenje – production of electric household appliances
Lek – production of pharmaceutical and chemical products
Krka – medicines, production of pharmaceutical products
Prevent – car-seat covers, protective clothing and gloves
Sava Tires – production of tires for vehicles
Impol – aluminum production
Talum – aluminum production

Industry

Over the last 10 years, industry has undergone considerable change in Slovenia. Previously, the metal and textile industries were the most important. In recent years, however, the chemical and car-manufacturing industries have grown stronger and now make important export products. The food-processing industry is successful in the domestic market as well in international trade with countries such as Croatia and Bosnia.

The number of employees in the industrial sector has decreased in recent years as more people are employed in trade, tourism, and other service activities.

▲ *Lek is a pharmaceutical company that makes medicines.*

▼ *Pepper-growers in northern Slovenia*

Agriculture

Most farming companies are run as family businesses. Wheat, corn, and barley are the main farming products. The farming companies also produce sugar-beets, potatoes, alfalfa, apples, and pears in large quantities. Much of the farmland in Slovenia is set aside for vineyards, which are an important part of the agriculture industry.

Much agricultural land is grassland, and cattle-raising is the main farming activity. Farmers produce mainly milk, meat, and eggs. Farms are generally quite small, but there are plenty of them across the country.

Tourism

Income from tourism is important to the Slovenian economy. Most tourism is focused in the coastal region along the Adriatic and in the mountains. However, increasing numbers of people are also coming to Slovenia to visit the hot springs in the spa towns.

▼ *White-water rafting on the Alpine Soča River in western Slovenia*

Slovenia has such a wide variety of landscapes and climates that it is ideal as a holiday destination, and many different activities can be enjoyed. The Slovenian Alps are popular among skiers in the winter, while in the summer, there are many hiking trails that offer fantastic views across the region.

▼ *Terme Olimia, with its indoor and outdoor thermal pools, is one of the most popular spa resorts.*

The most challenging peak for mountaineers and climbers is Triglav, the highest mountain in the country. The name Triglav means "triple head," who was a pagan god revered by the ancient Slovenes. He had three faces – one face that looked back to the past, one that looked into the present, and one that looked forward into the future.

The routes through the mountain regions are some of the most attractive walks in the country, passing through small villages, past lakes and ancient castles, some of which are open to the public. Those in Bled and Ptuj are well known. From the peak of Triglav, there are magnificent views of the mountain landscape all around.

It is just a two-hour drive from the Alps to the Adriatic coast. Although Slovenia has only a small strip of coastline, it attracts many vacationers. The coast is rocky, but the sea is good for swimming, particularly in the summer.

The many caverns in the limestone hills of the southwest region are a major tourist attraction. This region features hundreds of crevices, holes, underground rivers, and caves, some of which can be explored. The caverns in Postojna are world famous. This is also an important wine-making region.

The use of hot springs for healing purposes dates back to Roman times, and today the spas in Slovenia are becoming increasingly popular with tourists. The most famous spas can be found in Radenci, Terme Olimia, and Moravci, as well as Rogaška Slatina – Slovenia's largest and oldest spa town.

◀ *Hiking in the mountains in wintertime*

Nature

Slovenia is home to thousands of plant and animal species. The reason for this diversity is the country's location at the junction of four very different areas in terms of landscape and climate: the Alpine, Mediterranean, Pannonian, and the Illyrian-Dinar regions.

Vegetation

More than 50 percent of Slovene territory is covered by forests. The type of trees found in these forests depends on the climate and height above sea level. In the high mountain regions, coniferous forests dominated by pine trees are typical, but fir-tree forests are very rare. In the coastal region, there are many oak forests. In places with a hotter and drier climate, there are wild-pine forests. Along the rivers, which are prone to regular flooding, there are oak, fir, and beech forests. Lime trees can also be found all over the country, and were once a feature of every village in Slovenia.

Many plants and some animal species are now in danger due to pollution, deforestation, and the construction of settlements and roads. To prevent the situation from worsening, some areas are now protected by law. Approximately eight percent of Slovenia has been designated national parks, regional parks, or landscape parks.

▼ *The Slovene landscape is green with vegetation, including many types of trees.*

◀ The Triglav National Park covers an area of 325 square miles. Mount Triglav is located almost in the middle of the park.

▼ Weasels are among the most common animals found in the region of the Triglav National Park.

Triglav National Park

As well as these parks, there are 720 natural monuments, 34 national reserves, and 77 natural monuments that are protected. The largest protected area is the Triglav National Park, which covers almost the entire Julian Alps. Within the park, natural places of interest such as glacial lakes, natural windows (naturally formed arches), and caves are protected. Special attention is paid to the protection of the vegetation, which includes the Triglav flower, Triglav gentian, edelweiss, and several other plants. Some types of birds are also protected, including the capercaillie, the black cock, and the mountain eagle. Among the mammals found in this region, the best known are chamois (a type of antelope), ibex (a wild goat), and weasels.

Caves

The Škocjan caves in the southwest of Slovenia are known internationally, and scientists go there to study the limestone features. Škocjan has more than three miles of underground passages, and caves that are more than 650 feet deep. They are registered on UNESCO's World Cultural and Natural Heritage List.

▶ The salt flats at Sečovlje are home to diverse bird life, and are registered on the list of internationally important wetlands.

Animals

The vast and dense forests all over Slovenia offer protection to large mammals such as bears, lynxes, and wolves. Of special interest are the animals that live in the watery underground areas. These creatures have adapted to living in permanent darkness. The best-known subterranean animal is the olm, a type of salamander that lives in underground freshwater lakes in the limestone landscapes of the Illyrian-Dinar region. The olm has become a symbol of Slovenian natural science.

Swamps play a significant role in the preservation of some amphibians. These swamps are also used as resting places by birds that migrate to warmer places in the autumn. The most important areas for migrating birds are the Sečovlje salt-pans, stagnant areas of the River Mura, the Cerknica Lake, and the Ljubljana Marsh.

The symbol of the sub-Pannonian area of Slovenia (in the northeast) is the white stork, which likes to nest on chimney-tops and telegraph poles. In the River Soča, the Soča trout is especially protected. The Karst sheepdog, which is a good sheep and cattle dog, and the Lipizzaner horse, are well known all across Europe. Both originated in Slovenia.

▲ *Wild goats roam the high mountain slopes.*

▲ *The cave salamander is common in Slovenia's limestone regions.*

◄ *The famous white stork is a declining species, which breeds in the warmer climates of Europe.*

The environment

Rapid development in transportation systems has led to an increase in environmental pollution, including noise and exhaust fumes. The construction of highways is having a dramatic effect on the environment and interferes with and restricts the passage and movement of wild animals.

Today, environmental issues are taken seriously in Slovenia. Young people are involved in various ecological movements. They contribute to a cleaner environment through such activities as waste-paper collection, cleaning initiatives at home, taking care of the natural environment, and playing a role in reforestation, all of which contribute to a greater ecological awareness.

▲ *The Lipizzaner horse evolved from Spanish, Italian, and Arab stock that found its way to Slovenia. The horses are born dark brown or black, but turn white by the time they are eight years old.*

Environmental issues

Human activity can have a detrimental effect on the natural environment. One of the most serious of these is deforestation, when forests and woods are cut down. In towns, the air is becoming polluted, and in some places the water is, too, as waste is dumped in rivers. Streams and groundwater are also in danger in some farming areas due to the overuse of artificial fertilizers, various chemical protective agents, and machinery. In Slovenia, great efforts are made to maintain a clean environment, although a number of rivers and groundwater systems have already been polluted. Despite this, people are not always ecologically aware and do not recycle household waste, even though many towns provide special containers for this purpose. The construction of highways is leading to a reduction in farmlands and forests.

Slovenia in Europe

Slovenia is a peaceful country and it welcomes visitors from all over the world. It has a policy of peace towards all countries and has avoided the wars that have wreaked havoc in other former Yugoslav territories.

After its declaration of independence in 1991, Slovenia started to build stronger links with central and western European countries. Slovenia is strengthening its international position and its reputation as a democratic, stable, and successful European country. On May 22, 1992, it became a member of the United Nations. Slovenia contributes armed forces to UN peace operations and thus actively co-operates in preserving world peace.

Slovenia is also a member of the European Council, the World Trade Organization, the Central European Free Trade Agreement (CEFTA), the Organization for Security and Co-operation in Europe (OSCE), and a number of other international organizations. It also recently attained full membership of NATO and is campaigning for membership of the Organization for Economic Co-operation and Development (OECD). Among the basic goals of Slovenian foreign policy are stable, good neighborly relations with Austria, Italy, Hungary, and Croatia.

▲ A Slovenian representative addresses the Global Congress on the issue of senior citizens.

The Slovenian government tries its best to promote peace throughout the world. One of the key ways it does this is through the international organization UNICEF, which offers help to people all over the world who are suffering from poverty, hunger, and disease.

◀ U.S. president George W. Bush and Slovenian prime minister Anton Rop during the ceremony to welcome new nations to NATO membership in March 2004

As a responsible member of the international community, Slovenia co-operates in political, military, and civil affairs to maintain security and stability in southeastern Europe. It has also founded an international fund for de-mining (rendering land-mines harmless) and helping the victims of land-mines in Bosnia Herzegovina. These activities have already spread to the neighboring Balkan countries.

The European Union

The Republic of Slovenia signed an agreement to join the European Union in 1996. The negotiations for becoming a full member started in March 1998 and were concluded in December 2002. The accession agreement was signed by Slovenia and nine other new member states in Athens on April 16, 2003.

After the signing, the agreement had to be ratified by all 15 existing members of the union and the European parliament, as well as by each of the 10 new member states. A referendum took place in Slovenia, during which citizens could vote about whether or not they wanted the country to become a member. 89.6 percent of all Slovenes voted in favor of accession to the EU. The accession agreement became valid on May 1, 2004, and on this date Slovenia became a full member of the European Union.

▲ *The Slovenian president, Janez Drnovsek, casts his vote at a polling station in Ljubljana in June 2004, during the European elections.*

◀ *Slovenian children with scarfs showing the symbol of the European Union, celebrate their country becoming a member of the organization in 2004.*

Glossary

Celts A number of different tribes from central Europe, who had the same language and cultural roots.

Communism A policial system based on the principles of government ownership of property.

Concentration camp Prison camps where Jews and other minority groups were sent by the Germans during the Second World War. Many died under the harsh conditions there.

Habsburg Empire The land under control of the German royal family, who gained the thrones of several countries, including Austria and Hungary, from the late Middle Ages to the twentieth century.

NATO North Atlantic Treaty Organization, established in 1949 to work towards security and co-operation between the member states.

Orthodox Church The Christian Church in the East; it has several independent sects, including Greek Orthodox.

Slavs A large group of European peoples with similar languages. Individual tribes descended from the Slavs, including Slovaks, Czechs, Poles, Serbs, and Croats.

United Nations An organization founded after the Second World War to promote peace and economic development in its member nations.

Index

Websites

www.lonelyplanet.com/destinations/europe/slovenia
www.odci.gov/cia/publications/factbook/geos/si.html
www.dfat.gov.au/geo/slovenia
www.slovenia-tourism.si